I0796991

BLACK HISTORY Biographies

Maya Angelou

Izzi Howell

Crabtree Classroom
crabtreebooks.com

All words in **bold** appear in the glossary on page 23.

Crabtree Publishing

crabtreebooks.com 800-387-7650

Published in 2021 by Crabtree Publishing Company

Author: Izzi Howell
Editorial director: Kathy Middleton
Series editor: Izzi Howell
Editor: Ellen Rodger
Series designer: Rocket Design Ltd
Designer: Clare Nicholas
Proofreader: Crystal Sikkens
Production coordinator and prepress technician: Ken Wright
Print coordinator: Katherine Berti
Literacy consultant: Kate Ruttle

Hardcover 978-1-4271-2791-4
Paperback 978-1-4271-2797-6
Ebook (pdf) 978-1-4271-2803-4

Printed in the U.S.A./112023/PP20230920

Library and Archives Canada Cataloguing in Publication
Title: Maya Angelou / Izzi Howell.
Names: Howell, Izzi, author.
Description: Series statement: Black history biographies | Originally published: London: Franklin Watts, 2019. | Includes index.
Identifiers: Canadiana (print) 20200358502 | Canadiana (ebook) 20200358529 | ISBN 9781427127914 (hardcover) | ISBN 9781427127976 (softcover) | ISBN 9781427128034 (HTML)
Subjects: LCSH: Angelou, Maya—Juvenile literature. | LCSH: African American women authors—United States—Biography—Juvenile literature.
Classification: LCC PS3551.N464 Z663 2021 | DDC j818/.5409—dc23

Published in Canada
Crabtree Publishing
616 Welland Avenue
St. Catharines, Ontario
L2M 5V6

Published in the United States
Crabtree Publishing
347 Fifth Avenue
Suite 1402-145
New York, NY 10016

The publisher would like to thank the following for permission to reproduce their pictures: Alamy: Stephen Parker cover, Granamour Weems Collection 5, Everett Collection Historical 8, Everett Collection Inc 11, ABC/Courtesy Everett Collection 17; Getty: John Bohn/The Boston Globe 4, Smith Collection/ Gado 6, PhotoQuest 9, holgs 10, CBS Photo Archive 12, Gabriela Maj 13, Walter Bennett/The LIFE Picture Collection 14, James M. Thresher/The Washington Post 15, Karega Kofi Moyo 19, Grant Halverson 20; Shutterstock: meunierd title page and 21t, Sharon Silverman Boyd 7t, studiovin 7b and 22, photka 16, Joseph Sohm 18, Antwon McMullen 21b.

Library of Congress Cataloging-in-Publication Data
Names: Howell, Izzi, author.
Title: Maya Angelou / Izzi Howell.
Description: New York, NY : Crabtree Publishing Company, 2021.| Series: Black history biographies | First published in Great Britain in 2019 by The Watts Publishing Group.
Identifiers: LCCN 2020045834 (print) | LCCN 2020045835 (ebook) | ISBN 9781427127914 (hardcover) | ISBN 9781427127976 (paperback) | ISBN 9781427128034 (ebook)
Subjects: LCSH: Angelou, Maya--Juvenile literature. | Authors, American--20th century--Biography--Juvenile literature. | African American women authors--Biography--Juvenile literature. | Civil rights workers--United States--Biography--Juvenile literature. | Entertainers--United States--Biography--Juvenile literature.
Classification: LCC PS3551.N464 Z6947 2021 (print) | LCC PS3551.N464 (ebook) | DDC 818/.5409 [B]--dc23
LC record available at https://lccn.loc.gov/2020045834
LC ebook record available at https://lccn.loc.gov/2020045835

Contents

Maya Angelou

Maya Angelou was an American writer. She wrote poetry, books, and plays.

▲ **Maya Angelou performed her poems in front of many people.**

Maya Angelou wrote seven **autobiographies**. These books tell the story of her life and childhood.

This photo of Maya Angelou is from the 1970s. Angelou wrote many stories, poems, and movie scripts from the 1970s to 2014.

Which events would you write about in your own autobiography?

Childhood

Maya Angelou was born Marguerite Johnson on April 4, 1928, in St. Louis, Missouri. Her older brother Bailey called her Maya. Maya and Bailey were sent to live with their grandmother in a small town in Arkansas when Maya was three years old.

▼ Maya's grandmother owned a general store that looked like this one. She sold food.

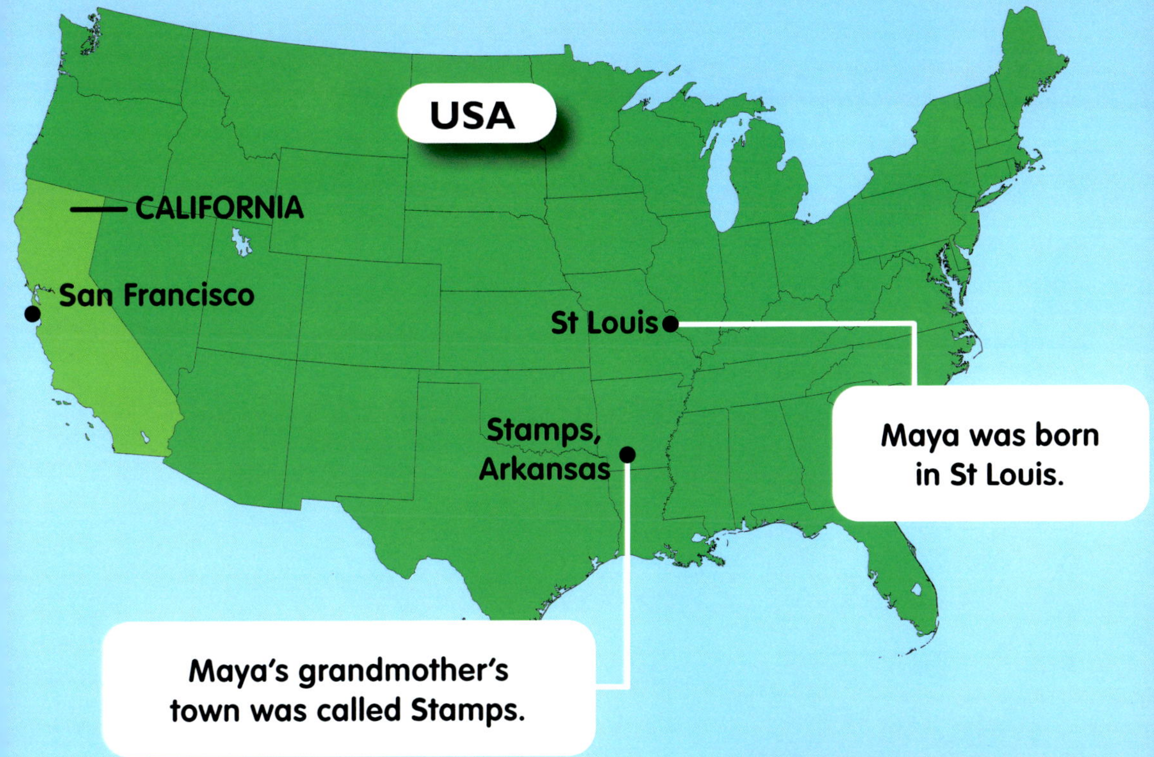

USA

CALIFORNIA

San Francisco

St Louis

Stamps, Arkansas

Maya was born in St Louis.

Maya's grandmother's town was called Stamps.

When Maya was eight years old, her mother's boyfriend attacked her. Maya stopped speaking for almost five years. A teacher named Mrs. Flowers helped Maya start speaking again.

▲ Mrs. Flowers and Maya read many books together. Maya fell in love with reading.

Racism

▲ Maya Angelou went to a school like this one, where all the students were Black.

When Maya Angelou was young, Black people and White people were **segregated**. They did not live together, and went to different schools, stores, and restaurants.

Some White people treated Black people poorly because of **racism**. People in Maya's grandmother's town were rude to Maya and her family because they were Black.

▼ **When she was a teenager, Maya got a part-time job as a maid, like this woman. The White woman that Maya worked for didn't treat her well.**

Early life

When she was 14, Maya Angelou went to live with her mother in California. She went to school and studied dance. At the age of 16, Maya got a job driving **cable cars** in San Francisco. She was one of the first Black women in the city to work as a cable car driver.

Cable cars still carry people around San Francisco today.

As a young woman, Maya Angelou worked as a dancer and singer. She sang **calypso** music, which comes from the Caribbean.

In 1957, Angelou acted in a film as a calypso dancer and singer. ▶

Writing

In 1968, Maya Angelou wrote her first autobiography. It was called *I Know Why the Caged Bird Sings*. It told the story of her childhood.

I Know Why the Caged Bird Sings **was turned into a film in 1979. These actors are playing the characters of Maya Angelou and her mother.** ▶

▲ Angelou signed copies of her books for her fans.

Maya Angelou wrote six more autobiographies. They tell the story of the first 40 years of her life. She also wrote poems, plays, movies, children's books, and even cookbooks!

Fighting racism

In the 1950s and 1960s, many people fought against racism. They wanted Black people to be treated the same as White people. Maya Angelou was friends with many famous **civil rights activists**.

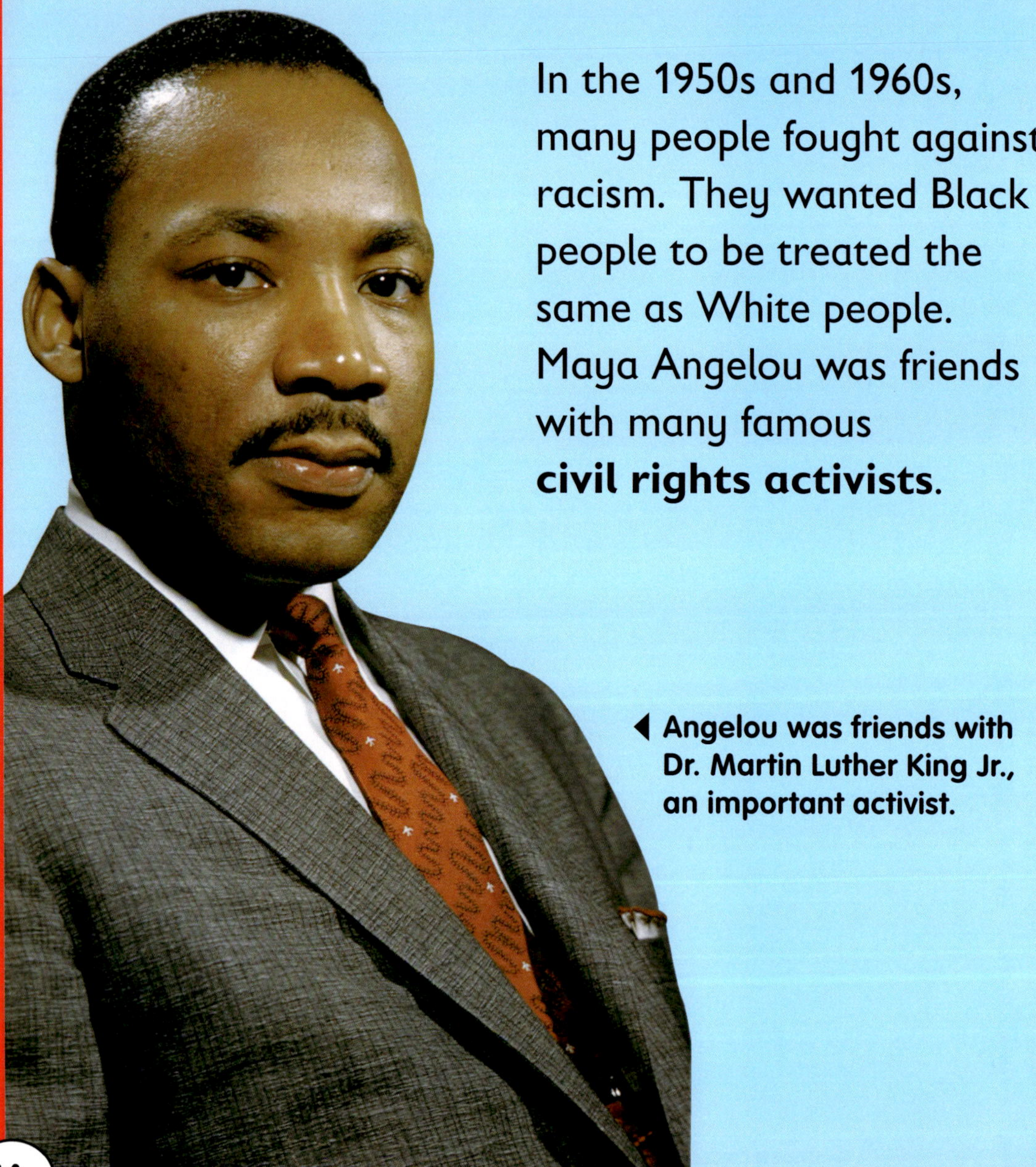

Angelou was friends with Dr. Martin Luther King Jr., an important activist.

Maya Angelou helped to organize civil rights **marches**. She also organized events to raise money for **protests**.

Angelou continued to fight against racism all of her life. In this photo, she is shown on a protest march in 1983.

Has your family ever been to a protest march or event? What was the event for?

Entertainment

For all of her life, Maya Angelou was busy with different types of entertainment. She wrote **scripts** for TV shows and films.

Angelou **directed** some films and TV shows. She told the actors what to do.

Maya Angelou also worked as an actor. She acted in plays, TV shows, and films.

▲ Maya Angelou starred in the film *There Are No Children Here* with talk show host and actor Oprah Winfrey.

Speaking and teaching

As well as writing, Maya Angelou shared her ideas with the world by speaking. She gave **speeches** and performed her poems out loud.

▲ In 1993, Maya Angelou performed one of her poems at an important ceremony to celebrate Bill Clinton's swearing in as president.

In 1982, Maya Angelou became a **professor** at a university in North Carolina. She taught classes about American history and **culture**.

▲ **Maya Angelou spent 32 years teaching at Wake Forest University in North Carolina.**

Remembering Maya Angelou

▲ **Many people came to a special event to celebrate the life of Maya Angelou after she died.**

Maya Angelou died on May 28, 2014. She was 86 years old.

Maya Angelou is remembered around the world for her work as a writer. Many people enjoy reading her books, poems, and plays.

This street painting in Montreal, Canada, celebrates Maya Angelou. ▶

◀ **Many people remember quotes from Maya Angelou, such as this one written on a sign at a protest in 2018.**

Quiz

Test how much you remember.

Check your answers on page 24.

1. When was Maya Angelou born?
2. Who gave Maya Angelou the name "Maya"?
3. Where did Maya Angelou drive cable cars?
4. What was the title of Maya Angelou's first autobiography?
5. Name two other types of text that Maya Angelou wrote.
6. How old was Maya Angelou when she died?

Glossary

activist Someone who tries to change society

autobiographies Books written by people about their own lives

cable cars A type of public transportation, similar to a streetcar

calypso A style of music and dance from the Caribbean

civil **rights** Rights that protect people from unfairness, such as the right to vote or public education

culture The traditions of a country or a group of people

directed Told actors what to do

marches Walks organized by a group to show they don't agree with something

part-time Describes a job that only takes up part of your time

perform To do something to entertain people

professor A teacher at a university

protests Events where people show they disagree with something

quotes Phrases that are taken from something someone has written or said

racism Treating people badly because of their race or color of their skin

scripts The words in movies, plays, or TV shows

segregated Kept separate by law

speeches Talks given by a person to groups of people

Index

Answers:

1: April 4, 1928; 2: Her brother Bailey; 3: San Francisco; 4: *I Know Why the Caged Bird Sings*; 5: Poems, plays, children's books, cookbooks, film and TV scripts; 6: 86 years old

Teaching notes:

Some children should be able to enjoy this book as independent readers. Other children will need more support.

Before you share the book:

- Ask what do readers already know about Maya Angelou?
- Introduce the differences between autobiography—a book written about your own life—and biography—a book written about someone else's life. Which type of book do readers think this might be?

While you share the book:

- Help children to read some of the more unfamiliar words.
- Talk about the questions. Encourage readers to make links between their own experiences and the events described.
- Talk about the pictures. How can you tell that some of the pictures were taken a long time ago, but others are more recent?

After you have shared the book:

- List all the jobs that Maya Angelou had. Discuss which were jobs that she might have enjoyed.
- Talk about why Maya Angelou was so interested in civil rights.
- Ask children why they think people today still remember Maya Angelou.